The missing eye

by Stan Cullimore

Characters: Narrator
Darren – the hero.
Bill – his friend.
One Eye – a giant with only one eye.
Big Nose – his girl friend.

Scene 1: On the deck of the ship 'The Wet Goat.' Late one night.

Narrator Darren and Bill had been at sea for a long time…

Darren You know what, Bill?

Bill What?

Darren I've just worked it out.

Bill What do you mean, worked it out?

Darren We've been at sea for one hundred and three days.

Bill It's no wonder I'm so bored!

Narrator The two friends had set sail to look for treasure, but so far they had not been very lucky.

Darren Who is going to do look-out duty tonight, Bill?

Bill I don't mind who is going to do it.

Darren	Good.
Bill	As long as it isn't me.
Darren	Bill, that's not fair. You never keep look-out.
Bill	That's because it's boring.
Darren	I know it is. But we will never find any treasure if we don't keep a look-out for it!
Bill	OK, then. I'll keep look-out.
Narrator	Bill yawned and rubbed his eyes...
Darren	No, you won't. You'll just fall asleep.
Bill	I'll try not to.
Narrator	Bill yawned again.
Bill	But it won't be easy.
Darren	Bill, If we don't watch where we are going we'll never find any treasure.
Bill	I know, I know.
Darren	And, we might just crash into something!

Bill	No chance! This sea goes on forever. We couldn't hit anything if we tried!
Darren	Well, I'm off to bed. Goodnight, Bill.
Bill	Goodnight, Darren.
Narrator	When Darren had gone, Bill lay down and closed his eyes. Soon he was fast asleep.
Bill	Zzzzzzzzzz!
Narrator	Suddenly there was a loud CRASH.
Bill	Zzzzzzzzzz!
Narrator	Darren came back up on deck...
Darren	Bill, wake up. We've hit something!
Bill	What do you mean, wake up? I wasn't asleep.
Darren	Yes, you were.
Bill	No, I was not. I was just thinking very hard.
Darren	You were snoring!
Bill	Only a little bit!
Narrator	They both looked over the side of the ship.

Darren	I think that we've hit a sand bank under the water.
Bill	How was I supposed to see that?
Darren	By keeping your eyes open.
Bill	But it's *under* the water.
Darren	So?
Bill	Well, I can't see *under* the water, can I?
Darren	Well, there is a huge great island next to it!
Bill	Oh yes, so there is.
Darren	I told you we had to keep a look-out.
Bill	I am keeping a look-out.
Darren	It's a bit late for that now!
Bill	I can see something on that island.
Darren	Where?
Narrator	Bill put out his hand…
Bill	Over there.

Darren Oh, yes. I can see it too.

Bill What do you think it is?

Darren I don't know.

Bill It *looks* like a very, very big house.

Darren Yes, it does. I think we should stay well away from it.

Bill I don't.

Darren What do you think, then?

Bill I think we should go and see if anyone lives there.

Darren Why?

Bill Because we will need help to get the boat off the sand bank.

Darren That is true.

Bill And they can help us.

Darren I still don't think we should go to that big house.

Bill Why not?

Darren   Because I am not sure who lives there.

Bill   Are you scared?

Darren   No.

Bill   Yes, you are. You are just a big scaredy cat.

Darren   No, I am not.

Bill   Come on then, follow me.

Narrator   So Bill and Darren jumped off the boat and into the sea.

Bill   This water is cold!

Darren   Very cold!

Narrator   Then they swam over to the island…

Bill   I wonder who lives in such a big house? They must have a lot of money.

Darren   Bill…

Bill   Come on. Let's go and have a look at it.

Darren   Bill, I really don't think that is a very good idea.

Bill   Why not?

Darren	I have a bad feeling about this place.
Bill	Don't be silly.
Darren	I'm not being silly.
Bill	Come on. Just follow me!
Narrator	Bill walked up to a big door in the side of the house. He knocked…
Bill	Hello. Is anybody in?
Darren	I really do have a bad feeling about this place, Bill.
Bill	Coward!
Darren	I think we should run away.
Narrator	But it was too late…
Bill	Did you just hear something, Darren?
Darren	Yes, I did.
Bill	What do you think it was?
Darren	I think it sounded like someone with very big feet coming this way!

Narrator	Just then, the door opened...
Darren	Oh, dear.
Bill	Perhaps you were right after all, Darren.
Darren	Now I really do have a bad feeling about this place.
Narrator	Standing in the doorway was a very big, very tall, one-eyed giant.
Bill	Er... Hello, Mr One-Eyed Giant sir...
Darren	What are you doing, Bill?
Bill	I'm just about to ask this nice giant if he can help us...
Narrator	The giant smiled.
One-Eye	Yes, I can help you...
Darren	Oh, dear!
Bill	You see, Darren. I told you there was nothing to worry about.
One-Eye	...and then, you two can help me.
Darren	I don't like this! I don't like this one little bit.

One-Eye   Please, do come in.

Bill   Thanks. Come on, Darren. The nice one-eyed giant has asked us into his house.

Narrator   The giant opened the door wide. Bill and Darren went inside…

Darren   I still have a really, really bad feeling about this place.

Scene 2 *A little bit later, in the kitchen of the One-Eyed Giant.*

Narrator The giant picked up Bill and Darren.

Bill Thank you.

Narrator Then he put them on the table…

Bill So tell me, Mr One-Eye. How can we help you?

One-Eye Well, it's like this. Big Nose is coming over for dinner tonight.

Darren Who is Big Nose?

One-Eye My girlfriend.

Darren Why is she called Big Nose?

One-Eye Because she has a very big nose.

Darren Oh.

One-Eye It's a very pretty nose. Very pretty and very big.

Bill She sounds nice.

Darren Does she?

Bill	Tell me, Mr One-Eyed Giant. Do you want us to help you make the dinner?
One-Eye	Yes, I do.
Darren	I don't like the sound of this.
Bill	Why not? We can help One-Eye cook the dinner can't we?
One-Eye	Sort of. You see - you two ARE the dinner.
Bill	Oh dear.
Darren	I said I had a bad feeling about this place.
One-Eye	I *was* going to cook a sheep for Big Nose. But I don't really want to cook any of my sheep.
Bill	Why not?
One-Eye	Because they are my best friends. I love my sheep.
Darren	Good idea of yours, Bill. To come and look at this house!
Narrator	The giant smiled at Bill…
One-Eye	You look nice and fat.

Bill Thank you.

One-Eye I think you will make a lovely dinner.

Bill You know what, Darren? I have a bad feeling about this place now!

Narrator Just then, the giant blinked.

One-Eye Oh no.

Darren What's wrong?

One-Eye I've got some dust in my eye.

Darren Shall I get it out for you?

One-Eye No need!

Narrator The giant put his hand up to his eye - and pulled it out…

Bill That is not very nice!

Darren But it may be very useful.

Narrator The giant wiped his eye and put it back in again.

Bill I wish he wouldn't do that. It makes me feel sick.

One-Eye   I'm going upstairs now.

Darren   Why?

One-Eye   I want to get into some nice clothes before Big Nose gets here.

Darren   Well don't worry about us. We won't run away - will we Bill?

Bill   No. We won't run away - not even a little bit!

One-Eye   I know you won't run away. I'm putting you in the shed with my sheep.

Bill   Oh rats! Now we can't run away!

Narrator   With that, One-Eye put Darren and Bill in the sheep shed and locked the door...

Scene 3: *In the sheep shed.*

Bill It's all right, I've got an idea. I know how to get us out of here.

Darren Not another of your ideas.

Bill But this is a very good idea.

Darren Well, I've got a better idea.

Bill How do you know?

Darren Because my ideas are always better than your ideas.

Bill What is it then?

Darren It's easy. All you have to do is help me get up on to that shelf over there.

Bill Good idea, Darren. Not!

Darren Then you wait until Old One-Eye comes back. He'll look for me.

Bill Then what do I do - run away?

Darren No. You tell him that I have gone to sleep, on the floor *under* the shelf.

Bill   What are you going to do?

Darren   I can't tell you. I want it to be a surprise!

Narrator   So Bill helped Darren get up on to the shelf…

Darren   Bill, one more thing. This is very important. You must tell the giant that my name is *No-one*.

Bill   Why?

Darren   Because I say so. Now just do it!

Bill   OK.

Narrator   They waited for old One-Eye to come back…

Scene 4: *A little bit later. Still in the shed with all the sheep!*

Narrator Bill looked around the shed at all the sheep...

Bill One-Eye is taking a long time isn't he, Darren?

Darren Shut up, Bill. I'm asleep, remember?

Bill I wish he would hurry up. These sheep smell funny.

Narrator Bill looked around the shed again.

Bill Did you just hear something, Darren?

Darren Yes, I did.

Bill What do you think it was?

Darren I think it sounded like someone with very big feet coming this way.

Bill You mean, One-Eye?

Darren Yes.

Bill Do you think he's coming back?

Darren Yes.

Bill	So do I.
Darren	Bill!
Bill	Yes?
Darren	Shut up.
Bill	OK.
Darren	Now do you remember what you have to do?
Narrator	Bill did not reply.
Darren	Did you hear me, Bill?
Bill	Yes, but you told me to shut up.
Darren	Just nod your head then.
Narrator	Bill nodded his head.
Darren	Thank you.
Narrator	Just then, the door opened…
Bill	Er… Hello, Mr One-Eyed Giant.
One-Eye	Shut up!
Bill	I wish you would all stop saying that.

Narrator   One-Eye looked around the shed.

One-Eye   Where's the other one?

Narrator   Bill did not reply.

One-Eye   Did you hear me?

Bill   Yes, but you told me to shut up.

One-Eye   Just point out where he is then.

Narrator   Bill pointed at the floor under the shelf.

One-Eye   I hope he hasn't hurt any of my sheep.

Bill   I don't think he has. He's asleep. By the way, his name is *No-one*.

One-Eye   I told you to shut up.

Narrator   One-Eye went over to where Bill had pointed.

One-Eye   I can't see *No-one*. Where is he?

Darren   Up here, One-Eye!

Narrator   With that, Darren jumped off the shelf.

One-Eye   Where?

Narrator	Darren landed on One-Eye's back.
Darren	I'm here.
One-Eye	What do you think you are doing?
Darren	This!
Narrator	Darren put out his hand and took hold of the giant's one eye. He pulled…
One-Eye	Stop that!
Narrator	But it was too late…
Darren	Got it!
One-Eye	Hey, I can't see anything. Give me my eye back!
Darren	No! You said you were going to eat us.
Narrator	Darren jumped down on to the floor.
Darren	Bill?
Bill	Yes?
Darren	Follow me. Do what I do.
Bill	OK.

One-Eye	I *am* going to eat you. Just as soon as I find you.
Narrator	The giant smiled.
One-Eye	I shall stand by the door so you can't get out.
Narrator	As the giant was talking, Darren went up to one of the great big sheep.
Darren	Come here, sheep.
Narrator	Then he got hold of the fur and hung on underneath it.
Bill	Do I have to do that? These sheep are very big - and they smell.
Darren	Shut up, Bill.
Bill	OK.
Narrator	Bill got hold of a sheep and hung on underneath it like Darren.
Darren	Let's go.
Narrator	By now, the sheep were so surprised that they tried to push past the giant and get out of the shed.

One-Eye	You want to go out do you, sheep? I'll just run my hands over your backs to see if I can find that horrible *No-one*.
Narrator	The giant let the sheep go. Darren and Bill got safely out of the shed…
Bill	Phew, we're out! Now what do we do?
Darren	We go back to the ship.
Bill	Good idea.
Narrator	Behind them, the giant was running around the shed trying to find his eye…
One-Eye	I'll get you for this, *No-one!* OW!
Narrator	He ran right into the wall because he could not see a thing…
Bill	Shut up, One-Eye!
Narrator	but he could still hear…
One-Eye	You horrible little men. You're trying to get away. Bring my sheep back!
Bill	No chance!
Darren	Bill!

Bill	I know. Shut up.
Darren	No. Look over there.
Bill	Oh dear.
Narrator	There was a giant walking up to the sheep shed. A giant with a big nose. A *very* big nose…
Darren	I think I know who that is.
Bill	So do I.
Bill	Big Nose.
Darren	If that *is* Big Nose, we are in trouble. Big trouble!

Scene 5: *Seconds later...*

Big Nose What is going on, One-Eye?

One-Eye My eye! It's gone. He's taken it!

Big Nose Who's taken it?

One-Eye *No-one*.

Big Nose What?

One-Eye *No-one* has taken my eye.

Big Nose Well if no-one has taken your eye what are you shouting about?

One-Eye Because I want it back.

Big Nose Stop being so silly.

One-Eye He was going to make the dinner for you.

Big Nose Who was?

One-Eye No-one.

Big Nose Well if no-one is making the dinner for me, I'm going home.

Narrator With that, Big Nose turned around and went back home. In a very bad mood.

Darren That idea of mine was a very good one!

Bill I agree.

Scene 6: *Back by the sea.*

Darren   We must swim out to the ship.

Narrator   So that is what they did.

Bill   Now let's get away from here as fast as we can.

Darren   We can't get away yet.

Bill   Why not?

Darren   The ship is still stuck on the sand bank.

Bill   Then we must do something.

Darren   Yes, but what?

Bill   I don't know.

Narrator   Darren put his hand in his pocket.

Darren   Hey! Look what I've got!

Bill   What is it?

Narrator   Darren pulled out the giant's missing eye.

Darren   That gives me another idea.

Bill Good. I like your ideas. They work!

Darren Hey, One-Eye! We are over here!

Bill Shut up, Darren. He'll hear you.

Darren I know.

One-Eye I'll get you now, *No-one!*

Darren I've still got your eye, Giant. Would you like me to give it back to you?

One-Eye Yes. Then I can eat you!

Narrator The giant ran towards the sound of Darren's voice.

One-Eye I smell water. You're in the sea, are you?

Darren Yes, that's right. We are in the water.

One-Eye Then I shall drown you!

Narrator With that, the giant jumped into the sea.

One-Eye Ow. This water is cold!

Bill Very cold.

Narrator A huge wave shot away from the giant…

Darren	My idea is working!
Narrator	...and pushed the boat off the sand bank.
Bill	Hooray! We can get away now.
Darren	Do you still want your eye back, Giant?
One-Eye	Yes, I do!
Darren	Here you are then.
Narrator	Darren pulled back his arm and threw the eye right at the giant.
Darren	Catch it if you can!
Narrator	The giant felt around in the water and got his eye back. He put it in...
One-Eye	That's better!
Narrator	just in time to see the boat sail away...
One-Eye	Rats! I'll have to eat something else for dinner.
Bill	What do you think we should do now, Darren?
Narrator	Darren smiled.

31

Darren   For a start - I think that one of us should watch where we are going!

Bill   You are right.

Darren   Who is going to do look-out duty tonight, Bill?

Bill   I'll do it.

Darren   You will keep an eye out, won't you?

Narrator   Bill smiled.

Bill   How can I? You gave it back to the giant!

THE END